To my parents, for their love and support

Happy Day Out in Toowoomba

Finn & Henry explore the town

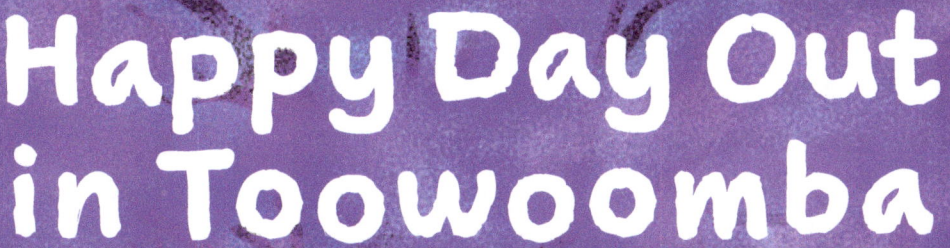

Author – Megan Carige
Illustrator – Laura Larissa Malishev

Happy Day Out in Toowoomba
Author – Megan Carige

© Megan Carige 2017

www.happydayout.com.au
happydayoutbook@gmail.com

This book is sold with the understanding that the author is not offering specific personal advice to the reader. Although the author and illustrator have tried to make the information as accurate as possible, they accept no responsibility for any loss or risk, personal or otherwise, that happens as a consequence of the use and application of any of the contents of this book.

All rights reserved. This book may not be reproduced in whole or part, stored, posted on the internet, or transmitted in any form or by any means, electronic, mechanical, photocopying, recording, or other, except brief extracts for the purpose of review, without written permission from the author of this book.

Edited and published by: Alex Fullerton www.authorsupportservices.com
Illustrated by: Laura Larissa Malishev

National Library of Australia Cataloguing-in-Publication

Creator: Carige, Megan, author.

Title: Happy day out in Toowoomba: Finn & Henry explore the town/Megan Carige; illustrated by Laura Malishev.

ISBN: 9780987615824 (paperback)

Target Audience: For pre-school age.

Subjects: Toowoomba (Qld.)--History--Juvenile literature.
Toowoomba (Qld.)--Description and travel—Juvenile literature.
Darling Downs (Qld.)--Description and travel--Juvenile literature.
Other Creators/Contributors: Malishev, Laura, illustrator.

Let's have a happy day together!

We have a happy time at Queens Park
in the morning.
We love to play around the big roller.

We are happy riding our bikes around
Prince Henry Drive.
Lockyer Valley, what a view!

We have a happy time running through the purple blossoms under the jacaranda tree.

We have a happy time spotting the big cats at the Darling Downs Zoo and hearing them
ROAR))))

We are so happy during spring at Laurel Bank Park.
We love going up high on the viewing platform.

We have a happy time on the steam train to Spring Bluff.
The flowers are so colourful.

We have a happy time at Cobb+Co Museum.
We love to climb in the old coach
and pretend to drive.

We are happy eating ice cream at Picnic Point. YUMMY!

We are happy during
Story Time in the City Library.
We love to pick our favourite books to read.

We have a happy time watching the children's shows at the Empire Theatre.

We have a happy time at Lake Cressbrook watching the sail boats.

We are happy hiking up
Table Top Mountain.
It is really high up there!

We have a happy time feeding the ducks at Lake Annand.

We are happy in the evening, at Picnic Point, watching the Australian flag with the big lights shining on it.

We are happy but tired driving over Mount Kynoch looking at the twinkling lights of Toowoomba.

We hope you had a happy day with us.

Tick off the sites you visited with Finn & Henry...

- [ ] Play in Queens Park
- [ ] Visit Prince Henry Drive
- [ ] Find a Jacaranda tree
- [ ] Visit the Darling Downs Zoo
- [ ] Play in Laurel Bank Park
- [ ] Visit Spring Bluff
- [ ] Visit Cobb+Co Museum

- [ ] Visit Picnic Point
- [ ] Visit the Toowoomba City Library
- [ ] Visit the Empire Theatre
- [ ] Watch the sail boats on Lake Cressbrook
- [ ] Hike up Table Top
- [ ] Feed the ducks at Lake Annand
- [ ] Drive over Mt Kynoch at night

About the Author

MEGAN CARIGE spent her earlier childhood living in Fiji before her family moved to Toowoomba. Megan has spent most of her adult life living, working and visiting cities around Australia and the world.

Recently moving back to live in the beautiful Garden City of Toowoomba with her two young sons, gave Megan the inspiration for her first children's story book, *Happy Day Out in Toowoomba*.

Megan's second book, *Happy Day Out on the Sunshine Coast* is now part of the successful *Happy Day Out* book series. You can see more by visiting: www.happydayout.com.au.

About the Illustrator

LAURA MALISHEV currently resides in Geelong but has spent many years living and studying in other parts of Australia. Laura works with children as an oral health therapist, and has always loved painting and drawing. *Happy Day Out in Toowoomba* has allowed Laura to indulge in her passion of colour, texture & light.

Happy Day Out in Toowoomba is Laura's second Children's book she has worked on.